On Earth As It Is in Heaven: Love

One

Thomas Eiseman

Table of Contents

4

Dedication

Thank you to my friends, family and all the inhabitants known and unknown! You know who you are! You are my universe and I appreciate you infinitely! Thank you profoundly!

Tend To Your Baby

Whatever garden you wish to grow, tend.

Disclaimer: Preface to the Preface

The words you're about to read are signs and
symbols that come alive in you anew.
The viewpoints you are about to read into
are not necessarily the same as what is trying
to be conveyed. I am not the author of the
earth and the sky, or the fish in the sea, or
the baby in the womb, nor did I design you
or me. So, the aim of this book is
awakening, a return home to the state of the
state and the source of the source that is
before your point of view.
The real poem is the universe and mine are
just an interpretation and translation.

Stop, look, listen and feel; find what is
before you and me, the place love calls real.
We live by story we deem right, whether it is
outlook or insight, but asked a million times,
"but why" we finally have to conclude it's a
mystery and sigh.

Thinking you know what is before, once
upon a time, your mind adds distance to

what is sublime.
You didn't hear it from me, for your tale
comes alive through you: look back and you
will actually find your tail is attached to you!

Preface

What I write about in this book is in common with all of us as a universe or cosmos. This life-intelligence-love that I refer to within these pages does not come from us, but through us. Our thinking creates a perspective, a point of view, which is merely an interpretation and translation of what was before we even had thought. Hence, in attempting to communicate through idea, thought, and language, we create one stance against another, and - with the aid of self-preservation and fear - continue to have conflicting stand points that will never end by debate or argument.

It would be an abuse of power to claim myself as the source of any power, or for me to label anyone else according to my side, position, angle, or belief. In my abuse of power, I would perpetuate the conflict of division and subsequent sides of debate, for in dividing this world, this house, I would continue to cause more problems, and my cyclical abuse of power would corrupt, yet again…

My aim in writing this work is to aid each individual in finding the unifying power of life-intelligence-love we all share; yet, we must also be careful, for so does the ability to both label and corrupt that power.

To be certain, this universe is not two, except by our perspective, and to find this truth - to find the right leader outside yourself - would be an endless, untenable task. The same universe within is throughout. No one can find this truth or place anywhere other than now, before you. In this realization, this uncovering of life-intelligence-love, time, understanding, and acceptance are one. Let this power flow through you in compassion and you will be guided in intelligence and wisdom.

Confinement?

Can you fit a song into a note or a universe
in a word or a mystery into a definition?

Can you confine life to "me" or God into
what "I" think? Can you define, by what
you thought,

That which is before you and me?

Is it but an endless debate to use thought to
try to explain the shortcomings of thought?

Can we ever explain what is beyond thought
and capture this present, this universe that is
eternally

Before you and me in thought?

Serenity

God grant us the serenity
to accept Your love;
the courage to share Your love;
and the wisdom to know
the difference between
Your will and our will, in love.

Look

Love is your timeless truth.
Look into the mirror and into your eyes.
This eternal essence flows out and remains
in,
radiant like the Sun,
vaster than all space.

Through Your Eyes a smile of infinite
Beauty and worth fills the universe with
Limitless possibility.

Look into my eyes and I will show you your
reflection.
Look into your eyes, your heart,
and find the light that lights all the heavens
and be found.
Being still I know you by heart!

Onto Eternity

Silence is the narrow path that opens,
As a garden,
Onto eternity.

God is love,
Such is His son,
In this eternal light,
God is one.

As God is one,
God has all the characteristics
Of all characters.
As God is love,
We are connected,
As below so above.

God is one throughout all time,
Eternal,
And no time at all.
God is one,
Throughout all distance
As essence,
And no distance at all,
As presence.

God so loves the world,
He for-gives this world anew.

Find this love supreme
In me and you.

For God there is no distance,
In time or throughout all space.
So be for God,
And light this Holy Place.

Amuse

Love your mind for it can create and amuse
in infinite ways.
It is your gift of perception, perspective and
choice of awareness.

The mind is pure imagination, creativity,
identifications and attitude.

When you learn to love your mind for what
it is,
You appreciate the whole world for what it
is.

Mystery

Before all time and history,
Timeless truth meets mystery.

And so the two remain as one
To join our heart within the Son.

Grace

Mystery and clarity meet to reveal beauty
and intrigue and by the grace of this
meeting, love.

The kiss of true love is received in the
mystery of now as a transfiguration. This
immaculate conception reveals a virgin birth
and in compassion, like the Son, we go forth
as a light unto the world for everyone.

As love we are a blessing to all nations in
perfect relationship as a universe.

Forgiveness flows naturally on earth as it is
in heaven and the fruit ripens on the vine as
you and me.

Painted With A Broad Brush

Reactions, because we care, painted with a
broad brush-for heaven's sake beware!

Writing and speaking with words can feel
like grasping at straws, but perhaps the
Words are like a mustard seed, as some day
the heart and intention will be heard, our
mistaken identity cured.

Words are food for thought,
Signs and symptoms from above,
Not divisive ways to be caught,
But to find our way to God above.

Not Two

Thinking is a process of I.
I am not the culmination of thinking,
But what I think is the culmination of I.
God and I
Can't the same place occupy,
Except by thinking, the process of I.

You can't serve two masters -
The master is either I or Thou.
The time is never then, but always now!

Frozen Id-entity

There's something rather than nothing
because thinking makes it so.

In addition, we divide and endlessly argue
armed with limited information, slant and
angle, thinking, believing, and point of view,
in the illusion of time and distance, in an
obvious no-win scenario.

Surely there is no thing until we take ideas
out of a context, a context that will always
remain a mystery and give these past events,
parts and particles, names and labels, and
make them something rather than nothing,
for no thing or part can exist without the
ineffable whole, but we insist and persist in
our belief in frozen identities.

Get To The Point

How do we get to this starting point?
We get to this point, like any point, by
making a point, defining it and labelling the
point, beginning.
As more information is discovered, science
broadens horizons - but religion,
Understood as rejoining in compassion this
world - is eternally paramount,
Foundational and complete.

Rational discussion is defined by what we
believe to be rational.

Religion refers to God yet science uses the
word universe or cosmos to describe what is
complete.

Give A Look

Look at yourself hiding in that shadow.
Rejoice!
Sing today with the universe,
join again this music,
dance with the cosmos.
The rain has light and shadow, but this day,
come out of the shadow and let the song and
dance that comes through you, free.
Today let there be light.
Let you be you and all parts be played with
nothing on, but grace.
Set free that which is; set free that which
you are.
Today dance with the sun, the moon, and set
your heart and mind free.
Rejoin love and be so pure that even a
deadman will know where we are!

Universal

This universe is life and life is this universe.
In and as life there is only now,
But this very present is in constant flux and
still remains absolutely coordinated.
This system cannot be confined, measured,
Since change is constant and there are
infinite variables to take into consideration.
In order to use the scientific method we need
repeatability,
Which cannot take place unless part is taken
out of context.
And as the whole, what appears to be
chaotic and/or random,
Simply indicates there's too much
information to process or measure.
A moving target or dynamic part taken out
of context,
A context that contains infinite variability,
Cannot be measured,
For the part is the context.

What Makes Whatever So?

Thinking, our thinking, makes whatever so.
Thinking is always based on limited
information. So, thinking limits our
formation and perpetuates our arguments for
ever.

Thinking leads to beliefs and beliefs form
expectations and expectations lead to dead
ends - unless we recognize our dilemma.

Who and where we are are made up of
beliefs, and the light at the end is our new
beginning or breakthrough to isness.

What is, I am and what am, is.

As Thee

One lives in relationship with the
environment and as the environment,
But as a result of basing our psyche,
community, culture, and world on stories,
We must either unravel these stories or,
Live before and beyond their confinement
and misinformation,
For they simply become prejudice and
prevarications.

Communication is rendered impossible and
remains so unless we take into consideration
both reductionism and holism. In other
words, the responsibilities of the individual
and the responsibilities of each layer of the
environment on to the whole must be taken
into account when diagnosing,
communicating, and understanding
individual, human behavior and the behavior
of the entire universe.

Beyond Sides

Give me a subject, but don't paint it with a
broad brush and there, beyond sides, you
will find the whole of us.

Beyond all the stories we are led to believe,
More walls, better infrastructure, changed
policies right or left, before us humanity in
common, In Love We Trust.

Epiphany

When there meets here you have arrived,
And when you meet the universe, You have
found your destiny,
And when destiny meets fate,
One finds God alone,
And one is found.

Virgin Birth

This moment is all new,
Original and unique,
But contains the same primordial sound.

The expressions of this moment,
Conveyed in words,
Refers to a place of mystery that wonder
pours from,
Not from the words,
But from within the state of this absolute
impossibility of now!

We get tired of the routine,
But in the midst of the mundane,
The axis mundi,
We discover an extraordinary awareness,
Finding the timeless soul spring eternal onto
universe.
Singing a new love song from the eternal
source,
Through unique arrangements of words and
sounds,
Feeling this presence,
Be-loved.

What We Miss

No matter how close we may be in
proximity,
Our mind and story can make us feel so very
far away,
Yet if we were able to travel in space far
away,
Yet we could still see the earth,
We would realize how very close we are,
How very intimate this life is!

If we open our heart and see this universe
insightfully,
We would be completely amazed in wonder
And if we were to travel far enough away,
Literally or spiritually,
So that we couldn't possibly see the earth
anymore,
We would miss every single inhabitant,
absolutely.

Eternal Truth

Does it matter when the timeless truth is
written?
Does it matter who speaks the timeless truth,
And what language or expression is used to
transmit the Word?
Do we need to find historical facts,
Relive the past in order to find the present?
Do we have to verify a story in order to
understand love?
How long will it take for us to reconcile our
differences,
Or to forgive one another?
Why does any of this matter when Love,
The Word, Truth is an eternal present.

The Beauty That We Love

The beauty that we love is this universe-
It's who we are,

Let it be what we do.

Comprehend Or Apprehend?

We rarely look at how deeply we are
wounded,
Even after we are freshly wounded
But instead we continue to divide our self,
Apprehend our self and punish our self.

Awake In

Open your third eye and imagine and feel
this:
Once upon a time, now,
An energy,
An intelligence,
An ineffable spirit- Love-
Gathers the universe in beauty,
Equality and compassion,
And such is the spirituality of our body
throughout the heavens,
Right before,
Transfigured,
Once upon a time is eternally now,
And behind the scene and the stories in
between,
Before a first or second expires,
HOLY COW!

Life is our Medium that is Wild at Heart

Poetry is love, art and life.
An interpretation, translation,
By heart, soul and mind.
An expression, impression,
By feeling and caring,
Forged and designed,
To share,
What we must be sharing.

Check Your Aim

You are the parable and the fable;
Now is your story of Cain and Abel.
Fear and gravity both hold your feet firmly
on the ground;
Be careful who you blame for the troubles
you have found.
Fear and thinking, like gravity, are neither
good nor bad,
But thinking makes them so.
Be careful who you blame,
Or what you think you know.

Compassion

The Answer is within, before any question
asked.
Perfect love is God alone
and this is within each and throughout
as the universe known and unknown.
As God is one, one will is done.
In this spirit, love casteth out all fear.
In this respect, we find grace in effect,
as Love
alone
the Cure.

Re-spect

We as individuals lead a double life.
One life as an individual in fear and another
as humanity in compassion,
But this duality is adjoined in perfect love as
God alone.

Thus, all our heavenly virtues and deadly
sins are because we are born with caring
And this natural state of caring,
Leads to fear,
And this fear can be overcome by another
natural state,
Compassion.

As God alone what should I fear and just as
the word universe indicates,
We are one transcendent, in the midst of
caring and fear,
By grace,
Let there be light.

Liberty

What is perfect is beyond thinking. So, there isn't a certain way that you can or should think because the way, the truth and the life, is beyond what you can think. Love is by grace and by this grace you are set free, not by the way you think, but by the love between you and me. So, stop arguing and set all the inhabitants, including yourself, as oneself, free.

Perfection

Before a moment can expire,
Before a judgment or desire,
God is one, perfection found,
In your heart, Holy Ground.

Face to face,
Once and for all we see,
This universe both wild and free,
By grace, we live in liberty,
Love alone, you and me.

Metaspiritual

God makes us able ministers,
Able to know, by heart, the spirit of
everything.
Not by the judgment of time, place and part,
But by grace
In love
The Garden's grandeur,
Eden's work of art.

Save Our Soul

Unless you find your heart,
Love,
And give Love away,
We will continue to not be able to afford to
care for one another.
Without love for one another,
As one,
We perpetuate our own demise.
Love is the root of all goodness.
Love has ceased to be the present which we
share.
We divide and conquer with guns,
bombs, endless conflict, inequality and war.
We have no choice and no time,
Love is always and only now.

Priceless

What is the cost of peace on earth, of grace
and peace in our heart?
How much does it cost for freedom,
And how long do I have to work to be free?
Will one day mankind be free and find again
our humanity?
Why can't we afford healthcare, to care for
one another?
How much does it cost to fight a war and
when is the price finally paid?
We seem to have it backwards - that
freedom isn't free,
But war is the price?
Living in the dream of aloneness of me,
I can never be free in this duality
And the battle that ensues for self-
preservation,
And supremacy.
Still, living in the transfiguration unto God
alone,
To freedom, by grace, love is known.

Is Fixed Fixed?

Rather than see the universe as a universe,
That each part is a universe,
Part and parcel,
We develop arguments by creating sides that
do not really exist,
And then paint each side of an argument
with a broad brush,
Not realizing that both sides are one,
And the same multi-dimensional psyche,
culture and universe.
We live as a whole and as parts,
And in living as parts we develop symbiotic,
And parasitic relationships according to our
mindset.
If you believe you are fully informed about
this new moment,
This universe and life,
Then how can I have a discussion with your
fixed mindset?

I Am What Am

Is the way, the truth and the life inside you
or outside you, or is it in our midst?

If God is one, where is God found?
If nothing is good but God alone, where and
when is God alone?

How did it happen that we called this
cosmos a universe and how and when will
we find it again?

The Sum of The Parts

Even with a recipe for a big bang or a
primordial soup,
The first problem you'll run into is,
Where do you find the supermarket that sells
the ingredients!
Then there is always the problem of,
Keeping that soup or big bang the right
temperature and consistency.

Other challenges include:
How much of each ingredient,
How long does it take to cook,
How long will it stay fresh,
How many will it serve,
And - in describing the recipe -
How should it taste?

My Life?

My life is not my own.
In the womb I never managed my affairs.
When did I become the person that I think is
me,
And how did I divide the world of thee?
Why this Word universe,
Who amongst us is afflicted with this duality
curse?
What makes me think I'm in a vacuum,
That I can live all on my own?
How did I develop this mysterious disease,
That we all have grown?
Yours is not your story all alone,
But a struggle or breakthrough,
Before history we're known.
We've been given a responsibility to love
one another,
To honor our father and mother,
And care for the whole creation,
As a beloved sister or brother.
Jonah, stop trying to run away from your
heart;
Return home and help bring us back from
apart.

Let There be Light

If someone really wants to contribute to this
world,
Devise an socio/economic system in which
success is measured,
Not by the few being exceptionally
rewarded,
But by how healthy and wealthy we can
make this world.
 A system that admires contribution rather
than extraction,
And our heroes are measured by loving,
And not by their personal accumulation of
wealth.
A system where our leaders are chosen for
empowering others,
Not for their ability to enrich their self.
A system that values life above money,
Rather than the other way.
A system of, for and by the people,
As company, whether at work, as a nation, a
family or any group.

Rise from This Sleep

Dust is most certainly dead,
for only by the wind is it raised from its bed.
Dust in the wind One will never be,
unless one is lost in sleep cannot see.
But as the wind, the Spirit that moves
enlivens dust.
I Am is eternal throughout all space most
just.
The man i festo is e mancipated from the
dust to the Sky.
In the Spirit of love from the earth to the
heavens we fly.
In every atom, the song of this verse.
Listen, One will wake from the dust and the
curse.
Rise from this sleep in the kiss of true love.
   Peace is found on earth as above.

Stake No claim

There is no neutral ground in the universe:
Every square inch, every split second,
Is claimed by God and counterclaimed by
man.
Thus, the Fruit of the Tree of Knowledge is
eaten by each
And as you eat so you are.
So, eat from the Word and before you fall
today,
Recognize the Word is with God
And the Word is God,
In every square inch, holy,
Every split second eternal.

Freedom Is Free From Tyranny

Money has no value except that which is
endowed by monetary policy.
Scarcity brings value to the dollar and
devaluation to life.
Blessed are the poor,
Not those that are enslaved, oppressed and
impoverished,
But those, by grace,
One free from this forsaken tyranny.
Money is granted free speech rights;
Therefore, so is the free use of bombs,
Guns, unemployment, defamation,
oppression, murder and poverty?
And so it unnaturally follows:
That if corporations are living entities,
Endowed by their creator with human rights,
Than corporations are gods.
How does the law grant greater rights to
money and corporations than to you and me?
How can I have freedom under this tyranny?
Freedom is free.
For by grace only
Is freedom granted
To you and me.
Only in love is there truth,
Justice and liberty.

After All

After all you say
And do, "what is"
Is still "what is"
And "what is"
Is always true.
Judge it not,
But if you do,
What is
You will most certainly
Misconstrue.
To save "what is"
From being in this state of dis-ease,
Return to "what is" by grace most pleased.

You Are The Sun

You are the sun,
For your essence is pure light,
pure love,
Charming the world vibrant and warm,
lustrous and alive.

You are the moon, Reflecting love, light,
Shining upon all the fairest reflection
For their eyes to brighten,
Their heart to open boldly,
And for their soul to awaken to blessing
upon blessing.

Quintessential

God is one.
Why do we create inequality?
Every moment is new and everyone is, too.
Every event unique and every person, too.
Which label for a part of God,
Which label for me or you,
Which label will fit, which label will do?

Judgment or forgiveness,
How do you find what is new?
By grace or label, which shoe fits you?

Art

Life is art informed by imagination.
How close can you come to the person
Or place before you?
In love this verse is always new.
Imagine this, imagine that.
Love is the Answer,
Love is where we are at.

In Formation

Words in form on wings,
In ways originally designed,
And new ways
And directions close and far.
The origin of words is the place of aloneness
trying to reconnect.
Heard, the words inform new places that
open the heart to love,
A new present as a universe, God alone,
originality.
The spirit of the Word is always
metaphorical.
This Love letter must be interpreted,
And translated,
And in the respect of life-timeless truth,
This love is the Word transfigured,
Before any form formless,
The Wonder of mystery,
Of a heart-mind joined in prayerful
awakening!

Amidst The Sky

On Earth as it is in heaven,
Throughout the heavens,
I can look afar with the telescope or space
travel,
As far as I can see this is all the universe
infinitely.
And with a microscope or a collider,
We can see parts throughout the smallest
space,
And within the universe just one sacred
place.

We seem to be closer to what is closer by,
But by heart we could be closer to what
seems farthest apart.
Some parts seem so far away,
Such as the sun or God particles,
But if this just wasn't one intimate space,
We'd have neither home,
Nor universe, nor human race.

As we discover our thoroughly thorough
connection,
We uncover God's immaculate conception,
Beyond time's deception,
Our soul is unified in purist perfection.

Clear With A Chance of Mystery

Communication begins with communing.
Every word we say or feel about life, Is not life,
But a light upon the way,
Or an overcast sky held above today.
There are infinite parts to a cosmology and to a point of view.
So, this deep dark secret, we, by fact, misconstrue.

Before you, always, parts unknown.
By Grace, love, God's image, God alone.

Don't argue over what cannot be said, don't cast a stone,
But be still and know, the servant shares the throne.

Don't wreck a perfect relationship, bring up the dead -
Only by love will we be fed.

Are You Listening

Originality and authorship do not come from
repeating the same word,
But listening in this new moment love is
found, felt and heard.
Every word, every space, can inspire and
incite, replenish and delight.

It is you that miss feeling anew in what
seems trite,
Try listening to find love, an awakening
insight.

This is not the same day, the same breath,
the same heartbeat.
Love is common and in common as this
universe, God alone.
But the sacred is not banal,
Find wisdom and insight,
Dawn happens, even at night.

The Shape Of Space

The shape of the stars are outlined by space,
Oxygen becomes the body,
Translated by distance as the human race.
What gives shape to empty space?

The interpretation, through imagination,
Of every trace.
Welcome to this new look,
Our present throughout,
This sacred place.

What gives life shape,
Time and meaning?
What I think is so,
Before what I think so,
I simply don't know!

Face To Face

If you really look,
You would really see,
Oh, you would welcome this very moment!
For you would realize your long lost friend!
You would start crying tears of joy, as never
before!
For this moment is the return of your
precious loved one!
If you really see,
Your loved one is always here in your heart,
Wherever you are!

Being

Before existence is the foundation of
existence, non-existence.
No one can capture what is before existence
or after,
For in our midst non-existence is the abode
of God alone.

Existence demands non-existence,
As the Garden demands Eden,
And life demands love.

The End Is Never Ending:
Only The Means Justify The Means

Quid pro quo, war never ends war,
But by war is never ending.

In a never-ending battle for power, security
and supremacy,
Fear is our enemy and our ally,
But by the grace of God alone,
We find the image of Love by which we are
known,
And only by this love will we ever atone.

Rules

We live in a world of laws and rules,
Culture and memes,
But unless we find the spirit
Of these ways and means,
We will be lost in power struggle,
Conflict and schemes.

Locked in a cell with the openings quite
closed,
No wonder you missed the universe in
which God proposed.

Cannot Be Said

The simple facts and plain truth about life-
this universe, is this:
This place is thoroughly an eternal mystery,
And cannot ever be captured by words or
history,
But is found as Love, by heart.

The mystery of Love is reincarnated as
artistry.
Don't just recite this universe,
Be the heartbeat and feeling within.

This

Love is like this: it makes the river flow into the sea.
Love is like this: it makes the clouds join together to rain upon the trees.
Love is like this: it makes the words that form sentences fall from the heavens through our heart and form the ocean blue and the garden green.
Love is like this: it radiates from the Son in compassion to join us all as one.
Love is like this: it shines from the Eye of the Beholder upon our night and day and frees us in his majesty, her grace in every way.
Love is like this: it reveals the poetry of the universe reflected in your eyes, the gospel of your smile throughout the midnight skies, and your presence - a countenance that lights the way between all our goodbyes.

Beloved

How do you know if this is true love?

Did you ever find a moment when you
arrived?
Did you ever have the feeling you are
found?
Were you ever grateful you are alive?
Did you ever find in silence the song of
sound?
Have you ever seen in the twinkling of an
eye the world anew?
Did you ever see wildlife in the midst of thin
air?
Or in your deepest sorrow how much you
really care?
How do you know if this is true love?

When you find yourself right where you are,
Right before your eyes, true love,
You'll know that you are found.

Love Used To Hide

Anticipation and imagination are often
wilder and more exhilarating than
participation.
However, love, what I see in my heart, at the
heart of all that I sense, is beautiful and
attractive.
My anticipation and imagination cannot hold
a candle to the Sun.
In love with the inhabitants is beyond any
dream I can dream up.
Love releases the deep blue sea from the
confinement of time.
From this angle, all angles are a gift and
every breath an inspiration and a miracle.
As I look into the sky I am overwhelmed by
your eyes and I must turn away or be
consumed.
Hearing a night sing or the birds at dawn,
your voice, I shiver at this compelling art
beyond art.
Just being alive in nature,
rain or storm, warmth or cold,
finally the fulfillment of the Kingdom of
Heaven.
The Earth reflects the Sun,
smiling so kindly,
connecting my mind heart and eyes most

valuable, trembling.
This love, although seemingly contained in a
brief moment or room, this love exists
before and beside me.
Strengthening resolve and resolution,
bigger than I could ever be,
this love is a universe filled with thank you
and gratefulness.
Love used to hide so cleverly,
I couldn't find love anywhere.
Then, one look into your eyes, I find you
and I realize, upon seeing your hiding place,
at heart,
I find you easily.
Just beyond my hiding places
one is found,
for I have been hiding you, in fear, all along.

Hallelujah

My soul and your soul are God alone.
I know everything within and throughout as
Universe, and yet many precious souls go
Through a lifetime, all eternity, without
Hearing even one compli-ment!

You, Dear One, listen well and hear me
Aow, forever and ever, in the fulfillment of
All time, for all eternity, I love you,
For you are love, God's image.
You complete God.
You are sacred.
God's only Beloved Son,
Heart of all Hearts,
Shines in your Heart,
And this is where I see you and
Know you by Heart.

Look, Listen And Feel

Listen to anger in pause and find fear,
The natural cause.
Listen to your story of hate and find quite
clear, the one same source, again, as fear.
Beneath the fear, before you, you will know,
Care, love, as one, by heart, by God, be still
and know.
On Earth, again, the Garden, Eden's will,
doth grow.
Won't you please be still and know?
All our emotions, thoughts, symptoms and
signs, connect us, as Love, as Fruit of the
Vine.
Only God alone is good,
Seeing rightly, a sacred universe,
One Holy Neighborhood.

What is The Meaning of This!?

What is the meaning of this?
What is the meaning of my life?
What is the meaning of life?
What is the meaning of what we do?
We assign lots of meaning,
None of which is true,
For before I assign a story,
Here I Am, Me and You,
This universe,
From the beginning till the end,
All is new.
Who am I, Where are you?
A label, a name,
The spirit of everything
We misconstrue.

Intimacy

Get as close to this place as you can and
know what love is.
Pay attention to this place so you can hear
the universe in the faintest breeze,
Feel the movement of song within a dark
room or see the light of the moon from the
other side of the Earth.

As you ride this horse you can see the horse,
But there's another horse that you are
forming in your mind-your heart,
Which horse is real?

When these Friends meet,
You are as close to this Place as you can be,
And One is found. (repeat)

Find Yourself

The great Maestro is conducting Her
Orchestra tonight for a brilliant performance
that promises to light up the night sky with
Meteor showers from Heaven
And other sacred music flow freely from the
wings of Angels,
She has invited You with all your skills and
charm to play along or just applaud,
But your attendance will appreciate
And You will hear songs the Maestro has
Designed especially for You :)
And at Dawn, Son rise, You will find
yourself dancing to Her new verses
that keep streaming from Heaven as Her will
and testament of Eternal Love :)

Impossible?

A magician uses sleight of hand to pull a
rabbit out of a hat,
but only the real magician,
the Beloved,
can eternally pull a universe
from no-where
and give it all to you!

Let It Fly!

The language of the Earth and Sky, nature,
Speak so beautifully all I hear in words
seems trite,
Till someone stands up,
And starts speaking from that same wild
place!
Someone lets their heart fly and I am right
there, drawn in,
don't just use words, this is your heart,
stand up and let it fly!
There are ways so eloquent, truly lovely,
that this verse is all about,
speak of this with your true voice and I feel
that way,
Stand up!
This is your moment, speak, Let it fly!
Draw your arrow back into that quiet place
and then let us have it,
Right in the chest, so we feel it!
Those aren't just words or mere
observations,
That lion comes through real struggle,
passion,
Stand up and let it fly in whispers and
shouts,

In nuance and roughshod,
Let love fly!
Are you alive!?
Is this your dying message?
Do you care?
Let love fly!

You

This book is inspired by you.
If you don't know who you are,
look in the mirror of your heart, mind, body
and soul,
Beloved Universe-Friend,
and find yourself once and for all
and once and for all eternity be found.
Find your one true name and be found.
Your one true name is ineffable, but I will
just call you, my love.
I am most grateful, my Friend. Thank you!

Afterword

Many times, as I sit in stillness, a word or phrase will come to me if I am quiet enough to listen. These words or ideas are often epiphanies expressing the spirit that seems to flow through me, not from me. To echo Plato's *Ion,* I feel as if I am a channel for something else. For example, one of these epiphanies prompted me to write down a particular phrase which I am very happy with: *Hava Nagila.* Not sure of its meaning, I looked it up and discovered this lyric means *"let us rejoice."* So, let's channel the heart and wishes of our ancestors: love and rejoice in this day!